ice pops

photographs
Lauren Burke

recipes
Shelly Kaldunski

weldon**owen**

inside

all about ice pops

In a rainbow of colors, ice pops are the quintessential summertime treat. Many of us associate ice pops with childhood: a frosty snack on a hot day, or the trophy for chasing down the neighborhood truck after school. Sticky-sweet fingers and stained shirts were the inevitable results. The truth is, few adults are immune to ice pops' charms, though some may have learned more refined eating habits.

Ice pops are just as magical as ever, and easy to create in your own kitchen. In their purest form, all you need to make the treats are a pitcher of fresh fruit juice, a mold, a freezer, and a few hours. With the new "instant" frozen pop makers, you can have your treats in just minutes, even on the hottest day of the year. Either way, the variations are as many as your imagination can conjure. Look to the pages that follow for creative recipes, shapes, colors, and sizes, perfect for any occasion.

This book offers a range of ice pop categories, from the simple to the adventurous: Puréed fresh fruit is transformed into vibrant, colorful pops. Melted chocolate or cocoa powder help create crowd-pleasing chocolate pops. Silky custards, infused with such ingredients as fragrant vanilla, spicy cinnamon, and tropical coconut, offer a rich selection of creamy pops. And new flavors delight grown-up palates, such as spicy mango-ginger, heady lavender-huckleberry, and cocktail hour–inspired sangria.

Whether you're looking for a sweet finish to a family barbecue, an innovative finale for a cocktail party, or a sweet snack for children after an afternoon of outdoor play, ice pops are easy and creative treats that never require a special event.

types of pops

You'll discover many types of ice pops in this book, from fruit-focused to decidedly decadent. After you try a few, take the recipes as inspiration, mixing and matching flavors, playing with layers, and creating your own combinations.

fruity pops

Perhaps the most familiar type, fruity pops start with ripe, fresh, in-season fruit, which is puréed in a blender or food processor or squeezed with a citrus juicer. Sugar and flavorings are added to create a sorbet-like base, then the mixture is poured into molds and frozen until firm.

chocolate pops

Chocolate ice pops are created in two main ways: either by dissolving cocoa powder into a dairy base, or by incorporating melted chocolate with an egg-rich custard. Both methods yield intensely chocolately frozen treats.

new-flavored pops

In contrast to the classic tastes featured in the earlier chapters, these recipes offer innovative—and often unexpected—flavor combinations using such ingredients as fresh herbs, exotic spices, and flavorful liquids. Some flavors, such as the liquor-infused pops, are best suited for adult palates.

creamy pops

Rich, smooth, ice cream—inspired pops start with either a custard, as with churned ice cream, or a mixture of yogurt, condensed milk, or other creamy dairy product. A variety of flavorings can be combined with the base to create a smooth, layered, or even chunky texture.

ingredients

Simple to make, ice pops feature few ingredients, so it's important to select the best. From the fruit juice, to the block of chocolate, to the jug of milk, be sure to seek out high-quality products for the most appealing taste and texture.

fruit Fresh fruit stars in colorful and flavor-packed ice pops. Some recipes will simply call for fruit juice; others will call for puréeing freshly chopped pieces; and still others will suggest warming the fruit in a saucepan to release and concentrate the flavors. Regardless of the method, seek out the highest quality fruit you can find, buying it in its peak season whenever possible. In a pinch, you can use high-quality, unsweetened frozen fruit.

dairy For dairy-based ice pops, creaminess is achieved through the use of a number of ingredients, including milk, cream, half-and-half, yogurt, buttermilk, and even rice milk. Use full-fat milk or yogurt unless advised otherwise, as a reduced fat content may result in an overly icy final texture. Use large grade A eggs, as fresh as you can find, to achieve the desired luscious consistency in the finished pop.

flavorings The flavoring options for ice pops are nearly endless. Classic choices include high-quality chocolate and cocoa powder; vanilla beans or extract; and a wide array of nuts. Fresh herbs, such as mint and basil, and dried spices, like cinnamon and cloves, bring exciting new tastes to the genre. Keep in mind that flavors can dull slightly with freezing, meaning you may want to err slightly stronger than you would in other types of recipes.

liquids The liquid ingredients that you choose for your pops will also affect their outcome. If your tap water has a pronounced flavor, consider using spring or filtered water instead. Tea, coffee, wine, and liquor can also deliver bold flavor to ice pops. Observe the quantities for alcohol, as larger amounts can inhibit freezing. Check manufacturers' instructions before using carbonated liquids in instant ice pop makers.

tools

At their simplest, ice pops require no special equipment. A bowl, a whisk, an ice pop mold, and a freezer are all you need to get started. Add a few simple tools, many of which you probably already own, and the possibilities are endless.

kitchen tools A blender or food processor are necessary for puréeing fresh fruit for fruit-based pops. If you don't have these items, an old-fashioned food mill is an acceptable substitute. A small saucepan, a sieve, and a wooden spoon are recommended for making custard-based pops and other flavored pops in which solid ingredients need to be strained. Beyond these items, a good, sharp knife, a cutting board, and a sense of adventure are all that are required.

molds & makers You'll be surprised at how many items in your household can be used for the purpose of molding and freezing pops. An ice cube tray, a nonstick muffin pan, or individual silicone cupcake cups all easily mold and release the frozen treats. Kitchen supply stores and online resources also carry a variety of specialty ice pop molds. These low-tech options range from traditional to whimsical shapes, including push-ups, stars, rockets, flowers, sailboats, and more. New technology also offers "instant" ice pop makers, which freeze pops in just minutes. Units such as the Zoku Quick Ice Pop Maker feature a unit that is stored in the freezer, much like an ice cream maker, bringing new convenience to making pops at home.

sticks & drip guards While you can easily eat frozen treats on a plate with a fork or spoon, for many, the fact that the icy dessert is presented on a stick provides most of the appeal. Old-fashioned wooden sticks are found at kitchen supply and crafts stores. Many ice pop molds come with sticks, which are secured to the molds to stay upright as they freeze. Some also include drip guards, which offer a solution to the ice pop's tendency to drip.

unmolding ice pops

There are two common anxieties when making ice pops: that the pops will get stuck in the molds, or that the sticks will slip out or freeze in an awkward position. Follow these steps for perfect ice pops every time.

cooling Cool custards and other heated mixtures over an ice bath before pouring into the molds. Fill a large bowl half full with ice and water. Nestle a smaller heatproof bowl inside. Strain the hot mixture into the small bowl and let the mixture cool, stirring, until cool.

freezing Unless your ice pop molds contain tops that hold the sticks securely throughout the freezing process, insert the sticks when the pops are partially frozen to ensure proper placement. Also, always let your ice pops freeze until completely solid before removing them—if they're not completely frozen at the center, you might lose the stick when unmolding.

unmolding Let the ice pops stand on the counter for 3 to 5 minutes. If necessary, run the mold under warm running water to slightly melt the pops and release from the molds.

Get Creative
Look beyond traditional molds and wooden sticks to have even more fun with ice pops!

Freeze ice pops in small juice glasses, silicone cupcake cups, madeleine pans, or other common kitchen items.

Use a variety of "sticks," such as decorative straws, bamboo skewers, or cinnamon sticks.

Use edible sticks, such as pretzel rods, chocolate-dipped rolled wafer cookies, or biscotti.

Follow the manufacturer's instructions for using sticks when using an instant pop maker.

serving ice pops

Serving ice pops typically means handing them to waiting hands along with a napkin. But after making the tasty recipes that follow, and waiting patiently for the freezer to do it's magic, you'll want to serve the treats with a little extra flair.

presenting The options for serving ice pops can be as casual or as festive as you like. For example, you can pass the pops on a tray at a backyard barbecue, or plate them individually in dessert dishes or bowls for a casual indoor meal. Small drinking glasses work well for presenting individual pops, and leaning them against the clear glass will showcase pretty shapes and colors and at the same time catch drips. For a festive party platter, arrange the pops on a bed of crushed ice. Pops made in small, attractive individual molds, such as single shot glasses, are just as pleasing served in their molds, allowing guests to remove the pops themselves.

There's really only one strict rule when presenting ice pops: Serve them promptly and provide plenty of napkins! Once the pops are out of the freezer, you'll have about 10 minutes before they melt too much to hold and eat.

You can always unmold pops in advance, and then put them back in the freezer on plates or a sheet of parchment until serving time. Commercially produced pops may last in your freezer indefinitely, but fresh, homemade pops have a relatively short lifespan. It's best to enjoy pops within 3 days, for the best flavor and most even texture. Fruit purées or custard bases will keep, well covered, in the refrigerator for up to 3 days before freezing in molds.

transporting Bringing ice pops along on a potluck can be a challenge. For shorter trips, add the pops, still in their molds, to a cooler full of ice, and close securely. Dry ice will provide a longer life. If you'll have access to a freezer and sufficient time once you arrive at your destination, consider bringing a sealed pitcher of the liquid base and your molds, and pouring and freezing your treats on your arrival.

fruity
ice
pops

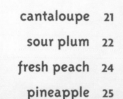

cantaloupe

Cantaloupe is a mild-flavored melon, so look for the ripest, sweetest-smelling fruit you can find at the market for the most concentrated flavor in the ice pops. You can also use honeydew melon in place of the cantaloupe.

4 cups (1½ lb/750 g) chopped ripe cantaloupe (from 1 small melon)

¼ cup (2 oz/60 g) superfine sugar

2 tbsp freshly squeezed lemon juice (from 1 lemon)

Pinch of salt

MAKES 8–10 ICE POPS

try this
To make ice pops in small baking molds as shown at left, see page 90.

In a blender or food processor, combine the cantaloupe, sugar, lemon juice, and salt. Pour in ¼ cup (2 fl oz/60 ml) water. Process until the mixture is completely smooth.

If using conventional ice pop molds, divide the mixture among the molds. Cover and freeze until solid, at least 4 hours or up to 3 days. If using sticks, insert them into the molds when the pops are partially frozen, after about 1 hour, then continue to freeze until solid, at least 3 more hours.

If using an instant ice pop maker, follow the manufacturer's instructions to fill the molds and freeze the pops.

sour plum

The pleasing sour tang of these pops comes from using firm, just underripe plums and not peeling them, as the skin is often the tartest part. If you prefer sweeter pops, use ripe plums and peel them before puréeing.

1½ lb (750 g) underripe red plums (about 7 plums)

⅓ cup (3 oz/90 g) superfine sugar

2 tbsp freshly squeezed lemon juice

Pinch of salt

MAKES 10–12 ICE POPS

Cut the plums in half and remove the pits. Place the plums in a blender or food processor. Add the sugar, lemon juice, and salt. Pour in ⅓ cup (3 fl oz/80 ml) water. Process until the mixture is completely smooth.

If using conventional ice pop molds, divide the mixture among the molds. Cover and freeze until solid, at least 4 hours or up to 3 days. If using sticks, insert them into the molds when the pops are partially frozen, after about 1 hour, then continue to freeze until solid, at least 3 more hours.

If using an instant ice pop maker, follow the manufacturer's instructions to fill the molds and freeze the pops.

fresh peach

This ice pop gets its delicious flavor from fresh summer peaches, which are sweetest from late July to mid-August. Other fragrant stone fruits, such as nectarines or apricots, can be used in place of the peaches.

3 ripe peaches, about 1 lb (500 g) total weight, peeled if desired

¼ cup (2 oz/60 g) superfine sugar

1 tbsp freshly squeezed lemon juice (from 1 lemon)

Pinch of salt

MAKES 6–8 ICE POPS

Cut the peaches in half and remove the pits, then chop the flesh. Place in a blender or food processor. Add the sugar, lemon juice, salt, and ¼ cup (2 fl oz/60 ml) water and process until the mixture is completely smooth.

If using conventional ice pop molds, divide the mixture among the molds. Cover and freeze until solid, at least 4 hours or up to 3 days. If using sticks, insert them into the molds when the pops are partially frozen, after about 1 hour, then continue to freeze until solid, at least 3 more hours.

If using an instant ice pop maker, follow the manufacturer's instructions to fill the molds and freeze the pops.

pineapple

When choosing a ripe pineapple at the market, look for a golden yellow color around the base of the fruit. The further the yellow color travels up towards the crown, and the more fragrant the fruit, the sweeter the pineapple will be.

1 pineapple, about 3½ lb (1.75 kg), peeled

½ cup (4 oz/125 g) sugar

Pinch of salt

MAKES 10–12 ICE POPS

pop swap
For a pineapple-banana-orange ice pop, replace the water with freshly squeezed orange juice and add 1 peeled banana to the blender or food processor when puréeing the pineapple.

Cut the pineapple into quarters and remove the core. Chop the flesh. You should have about 4 cups (1½ lb/750 g).

In a saucepan, combine the pineapple, sugar, and salt. Pour in ½ cup (4 fl oz/125 ml) water. Bring to a boil over medium-high heat and cook, stirring occasionally, until the sugar has completely dissolved and the pineapple has absorbed some of the syrup, about 5 minutes. Remove from the heat and let cool to room temperature.

Pour the pineapple mixture into a blender or food processor. Process until very smooth.

If using conventional ice pop molds, divide the mixture among the molds. Cover and freeze until solid, at least 4 hours or up to 3 days. If using sticks, insert them into the molds when the pops are partially frozen, after about 1 hour, then continue to freeze until solid, at least 3 more hours.

If using an instant ice pop maker, follow the manufacturer's instructions to fill the molds and freeze the pops.

blueberry–lemon verbena

Lemon verbena is a fragrant herb with a pure lemon essence. Seek it out at a farmers' market or a friend's garden at the peak of summer. If necessary, substitute 1 lemongrass stalk, trimmed and cut into pieces.

⅓ cup (3 oz/90 g) sugar

4 sprigs lemon verbena, each about 2 inches (5 cm) long

½ tsp finely grated lemon zest

1 tbsp freshly squeezed lemon juice

2½ cups (10 oz/315 g) blueberries

Pinch of salt

MAKES 8–10 ICE POPS

In a small saucepan, combine the sugar, lemon verbena, and ½ cup (4 fl oz/125 ml) water. Bring to a boil over medium-high heat, stirring occasionally until the sugar has completely dissolved and a syrup has formed. Remove from the heat and let cool to room temperature.

Strain the cooled syrup into a blender or food processor, discarding the lemon verbena. Add the lemon zest and juice, blueberries, and salt and process until very smooth.

If using conventional ice pop molds, divide the mixture among the molds. Cover and freeze until solid, at least 4 hours or up to 3 days. If using sticks, insert them into the molds when the pops are partially frozen, after about 1 hour, then continue to freeze until solid, at least 3 more hours.

If using an instant ice pop maker, follow the manufacturer's instructions to fill the molds and freeze the pops.

tangerine-bergamot

Bergamot, a citrus fruit grown in Southeast Asia and Italy, is commonly used to flavor Earl Grey tea. For this recipe, look for a tea that lists natural or pure bergamot oil as an ingredient which will lend the most pronounced flavor.

¼ cup (2 oz/60 g) sugar

1 bag Earl Grey tea with bergamot (see Note)

1½ lb (750 g) tangerines (from about 8 tangerines)

1½ tsp freshly squeezed lemon juice

Pinch of salt

MAKES 6–8 ICE POPS

In a small saucepan, combine the sugar and ½ cup (4 fl oz/125 ml) water. Bring to a boil over medium-high heat, stirring occasionally until the sugar has completely dissolved and a syrup has formed. Remove the pan from the heat, add the tea bag, and let cool to room temperature.

Meanwhile, finely grate the zest from 1 tangerine. Extract the juice from all the tangerines. You should have about 1½ cups (12 fl oz/375 ml). Pour into a 2-cup (16–fl oz/500-ml) measure with a pour spout. Stir in the zest, lemon juice, and salt. Stir in the cooled syrup, squeezing the tea bag to extract all the liquid.

If using conventional ice pop molds, divide the mixture among the molds. Cover and freeze until solid, at least 4 hours or up to 3 days. If using sticks, insert them into the molds when the pops are partially frozen, after about 1 hour, then continue to freeze until solid, at least 3 more hours.

If using an instant ice pop maker, follow the manufacturer's instructions to fill the molds and freeze the pops.

ALSO SHOWN: RASPBERRY-MINT AND LEMON-BUTTERMILK ICE POPS (PAGES 30–31)

raspberry-mint

Not as common as spearmint, peppermint adds a bracing quality to these ice pops. It can be found at specialty or farmers' markets. If peppermint is unavailable, fresh spearmint leaves or ⅛ tsp peppermint extract can be used.

4 cups (1 lb/500 g) raspberries

¼ cup (2 oz/60 g) plus 1 tbsp superfine sugar

¼ cup (⅓ oz/10 g) fresh peppermint leaves

Pinch of salt

MAKES 6–8 ICE POPS

In a blender or food processor, combine the raspberries, sugar, peppermint leaves, and salt. Pour in ¼ cup (2 fl oz/60 ml) water. Process until completely smooth. Strain the raspberry mixture through a fine-mesh sieve set over a large liquid measuring cup or bowl. Discard the raspberry seeds and peppermint leaves.

If using conventional ice pop molds, divide the mixture among the molds. Cover and freeze until solid, at least 4 hours or up to 3 days. If using sticks, insert them into the molds when the pops are partially frozen, after about 1 hour, then continue to freeze until solid, at least 3 more hours.

If using an instant ice pop maker, follow the manufacturer's instructions to fill the molds and freeze the pops.

lemon-buttermilk

Buttermilk brings a refreshing tang and creamy texture to these intensely lemony ice pops. If you don't have it on hand, whole-milk plain yogurt can be substituted for the buttermilk to achieve a similar flavor.

1 tbsp finely grated lemon zest

2 tbsp freshly squeezed lemon juice

1/2 cup (3 1/2 oz/105 g) superfine sugar

2 3/4 cups (22 fl oz/ 680 ml) buttermilk

Pinch of salt

MAKES 10–12 ICE POPS

In a bowl or large liquid measuring cup, stir together the lemon zest and juice and the sugar until the sugar has completely dissolved. Stir in the buttermilk and salt.

If using conventional ice pop molds, divide the mixture among the molds. Cover and freeze until solid, at least 4 hours or up to 3 days. If using sticks, insert them into the molds when the pops are partially frozen, after about 1 hour, then continue to freeze until solid, at least 3 more hours.

If using an instant ice pop maker, follow the manufacturer's instructions to fill the molds and freeze the pops.

mango-ginger

The sweetness of mango mingled with the subtle spicy flavor of ginger make a refreshing pairing in this ice pop. Simmering the ginger in a sugar syrup mellows the peppery bite and lime juice adds vibrancy.

⅓ cup (3 oz/90 g) sugar

½ tsp grated peeled fresh ginger

2 ripe mangoes, about 1¾ lb (875 g) total weight

2 tbsp freshly squeezed lime juice

Pinch of salt

MAKES 8–10 ICE POPS

In a small saucepan, combine the sugar, ginger, and ½ cup (4 fl oz/125 ml) water. Bring to a boil over medium-high heat, stirring occasionally until the sugar has completely dissolved and syrup has formed. Remove from the heat and let cool to room temperature.

Peel each mango and cut the flesh from the pits, discarding the pits. Chop the flesh and place in a blender or food processor. Add the lime juice, salt, and the cooled ginger syrup and process until very smooth.

If using conventional ice pop molds, divide the mixture among the molds. Cover and freeze until solid, at least 4 hours or up to 3 days. If using sticks, insert them into the molds when the pops are partially frozen, after about 1 hour, then continue to freeze until solid, at least 3 more hours.

If using an instant ice pop maker, follow the manufacturer's instructions to fill the molds and freeze the pops.

pink lemonade

This ice pop is perfect for a hot summer day. Just 2 strawberries blended into the lemonade create the signature pink hue and add a strawberry essence without compromising the bright lemon flavor.

1 tsp finely grated lemon zest

½ cup (4 fl oz/125 ml) freshly squeezed lemon juice (from about 4 lemons)

½ cup (3½ oz/105 g) plus 2 tbsp superfine sugar

2 fresh or frozen strawberries, hulled

Pinch of salt

MAKES 9–11 ICE POPS

try this
To make ice pops in small drinking glasses as shown at right, see page 90.

In a blender or food processor, combine the lemon zest and juice and the sugar. Pour in 1¾ cups (14 fl oz/430 ml) water. Add the strawberries and salt and blend until the mixture is smooth and pink.

If using conventional ice pop molds, divide the mixture among the molds. Cover and freeze until solid, at least 4 hours or up to 3 days. If using sticks, insert them into the molds when the pops are partially frozen, after about 1 hour, then continue to freeze until solid, at least 3 more hours.

If using an instant ice pop maker, follow the manufacturer's instructions to fill the molds and freeze the pops.

blood orange

Closely related to the navel orange, this crimson-colored cousin is available from December through May. Since they can be hard to find, it's a good idea to buy extra blood oranges and freeze the juice to enjoy beyond the peak season.

2 cups (16 fl oz/500 ml) freshly squeezed blood orange juice (from about 10 medium oranges)

⅓ cup (4 oz/125 g) pale clover honey

Pinch of salt

MAKES 10–12 ICE POPS

In a bowl or large measuring cup, stir together the blood orange juice, honey, and salt. Pour in ¾ cup (6 fl oz/180 ml) water and stir to combine.

If using conventional ice pop molds, divide the mixture among the molds. Cover and freeze until solid, at least 4 hours or up to 3 days. If using sticks, insert them into the molds when the pops are partially frozen, after about 1 hour, then continue to freeze until solid, at least 3 more hours.

If using an instant ice pop maker, follow the manufacturer's instructions to fill the molds and freeze the pops.

watermelon-lime

The thirst-quenching Mexican drink called *agua fresca*, a mixture of fruit, water, and sugar, is the inspiration for these layered ice pops. The base layer is made from the melon rind, which delivers a pleasant tartness at the end of the pop.

½ small watermelon, about 2 lb (1 kg)

4 tsp plus 3 tbsp superfine sugar

2 tsp plus 2 tbsp freshly squeezed lime juice

Pinch of salt

MAKES 10–12 ICE POPS

Scoop the flesh from the watermelon and remove any seeds. Reserve the rind. Chop the watermelon flesh; you should have about 4 cups (24 oz/750 g). Set aside.

Using a vegetable peeler, remove the fibrous, dark green peel from the reserved rind and then chop the rind; you should have about 1½ cups (7½ oz/235 g). Place in a blender or food processor. Add the 4 tsp sugar and 2 tsp lime juice. Pour in ⅓ cup (3 fl oz/80 ml) water. Process until the mixture is completely smooth. Transfer to a large glass measuring cup.

In the blender or food processor, combine the watermelon flesh, the remaining 3 tbsp sugar, the remaining 2 tbsp lime juice, and salt and blend until smooth.

If using conventional ice pop molds, divide the watermelon flesh mixture among ice pop molds, filling them three-fourths full. Freeze until partially frozen, about 1 hour. If using sticks, insert them at this point. Top with the watermelon rind mixture, filling the molds until full. Cover and freeze until solid, at least 3 hours or up to 3 days.

If using an instant ice pop maker, follow the manufacturer's instructions to fill the molds and freeze the pops.

rhubarb

Rhubarb cooked in a sugar syrup and then puréed creates an unexpectedly creamy pop, even though there's no cream in this recipe. You can decrease the amount of sugar by a few tablespoons if you prefer pops that are more tart.

1½ lb (750 g) rhubarb

2¼ cups (18 oz/560 g) sugar

Pinch of salt

MAKES 10–12 ICE POPS

Trim the rhubarb stalks and then cut into ½-inch (12-mm) pieces.

In a saucepan, combine the sugar and 1½ cups (12 fl oz/375 ml) water. Bring to a boil over medium-high heat and stir until the sugar has dissolved. Add the rhubarb and salt and cook, stirring occasionally, until the rhubarb has softened, about 5 minutes. Remove the mixture from heat and let cool to room temperature.

Pour the rhubarb mixture into a blender or food processor and process until very smooth.

If using conventional ice pop molds, divide the mixture among the molds. Cover and freeze until solid, at least 4 hours or up to 3 days. If using sticks, insert them into the molds when the pops are partially frozen, after about 1 hour, then continue to freeze until solid, at least 3 more hours.

If using an instant ice pop maker, follow the manufacturer's instructions to fill the molds and freeze the pops.

chocolate ice pops

classic fudge

That rich chocolate ice pop you remember from childhood is re-created in this recipe. The subtle milkshake-like taste comes from malted milk powder, which also helps keep the texture of the pops soft and creamy.

1¾ cups (14 fl oz/430 ml) half-and-half

1 tbsp unsweetened cocoa powder

2 tbsp malted milk powder

1 tbsp light corn syrup

½ tsp vanilla extract

Pinch of salt

4 oz (125 g) semisweet chocolate, finely chopped

MAKES 6–9 ICE POPS

In a saucepan, combine the half-and-half, cocoa powder, malted milk powder, corn syrup, vanilla, and salt. Bring to a simmer over medium-high heat, stirring occasionally, and cook until the cocoa and milk powder have completely dissolved. Remove the mixture from the heat and add the chopped chocolate. Stir until the chocolate has completely melted. Let cool to room temperature.

If using conventional ice pop molds, divide the mixture among the molds. Cover and freeze until solid, at least 4 hours or up to 3 days. If using sticks, insert them into the molds when the pops are partially frozen, after about 1 hour, then continue to freeze until solid, at least 3 more hours.

If using an instant ice pop maker, follow the manufacturer's instructions to fill the molds and freeze the pops.

chocolate-vanilla swirl

Offering the best of both flavors, chocolate and vanilla intertwine in this ice pop. Yogurt lends a refreshing and tangy flavor to this recipe. You may just find this ice pop refreshing enough to eat more than one at a sitting.

2 oz (60 g) bittesweet chocolate, finely chopped

1 tbsp unsweetened cocoa powder

¼ cup (2 fl oz/60 ml) heavy cream

1 tbsp light corn syrup

3 cups (24 oz/750 g) plain whole-milk yogurt

⅓ cup (30 oz/90 g) plus 1 tbsp superfine sugar

2 tsp vanilla extract

MAKES 8–10 ICE POPS

try this
To make bar-shaped pops as shown at right, see page 90.

In a heatproof bowl, combine the chopped chocolate, cocoa powder, heavy cream, and corn syrup. Set the bowl over (not touching) simmering water in a saucepan and cook, stirring occasionally, until the chocolate has melted, about 10 minutes. Remove the bowl from the heat and stir in 1½ cups (12 oz/375 g) of the yogurt. Let cool to room temperature.

Meanwhile, in another bowl, stir together the remaining 1½ cups yogurt, the sugar, and vanilla.

If using conventional ice pop molds, spoon 2 tbsp of the chocolate mixture into each mold. Top with 2 tbsp of the vanilla mixture. Add another 2 tbsp of the chocolate mixture and then another 2 tbsp of the vanilla mixture. Continue layering until the molds are full. Dip a paring knife into each mold and make a few figure-eight motions to swirl the flavors together. Cover and freeze until solid, at least 4 hours or up to 3 days. If using sticks, insert them into the molds when the pops are partially frozen, after about 1 hour, then continue to freeze until solid, at least 3 more hours.

If using an instant ice pop maker, follow the manufacturer's instructions to fill the molds, layering the mixtures as above, and freeze the pops.

double chocolate swirl

1 cup (8 fl oz/250 ml)
heavy cream

1 cup (8 fl oz/250 ml)
whole milk

4 large egg yolks

½ cup (4 oz/125 g) sugar

1 tbsp unsweetened
cocoa powder

1 tsp vanilla extract

Pinch of salt

2 oz (60 g) bittersweet
chocolate, finely
chopped

2 oz (60 g) milk
chocolate, finely
chopped

MAKES 10–12 ICE POPS

In a heavy saucepan over medium-high heat, combine the cream and milk.
Heat, stirring occasionally, until the mixture barely comes to a simmer.
In a heatproof bowl, whisk together the egg yolks, sugar, cocoa powder,
vanilla, and salt until doubled in volume, about 2 minutes. Slowly pour
about half of the warm cream mixture into the egg mixture, whisking until
smooth. Pour the mixture into the saucepan and place over medium heat.
Cook, stirring with a wooden spoon, until the mixture thickens enough to
coat the back of the spoon, 1–2 minutes. Do not let it boil.

Strain the mixture through a fine-mesh sieve, dividing it evenly between
2 bowls. Add the bittersweet chocolate to 1 bowl and the milk chocolate
to the other bowl and stir each until the chocolates have melted. Cool
completely over ice baths (page 14).

If using conventional ice pop molds, spoon 2 tbsp of the bittersweet
chocolate mixture into each mold. Top each with an equal amount of
the milk chocolate mixture. Continue layering the two chocolate mixtures
until the molds are full. Dip a paring knife into each mold and make a
few figure-eight motions to swirl the flavors together. Cover and freeze
until solid, at least 4 hours or up to 3 days. If using sticks, insert them into
the molds when the pops are partially frozen, after about 1 hour, then
continue to freeze until solid, at least 3 more hours.

If using an instant ice pop maker, follow the manufacturer's instructions
to fill the molds, layering the mixtures as above, and freeze the pops.

chocolate truffle chunk

½ cup (4 fl oz/125 ml) heavy cream

1 tbsp light corn syrup

8 oz (250 g) semisweet chocolate, finely chopped

1¾ cups (14 fl oz/430 ml) half-and-half

2 tbsp unsweetened cocoa powder

¼ cup (1.1 oz/32 g) malted milk powder

4 large egg yolks

⅓ cup (3 oz/90 g) sugar

1 tsp vanilla extract

Pinch of salt

MAKES 8–10 ICE POPS

In a heavy saucepan over medium-high heat, combine the cream and corn syrup. Heat, stirring occasionally, until the mixture barely comes to a simmer. Remove from the heat, add the chocolate, and stir until completely melted. Transfer to a small bowl and refrigerate until firm to the touch, about 1 hour.

In another saucepan, combine the half-and-half, cocoa powder, and malted milk powder. Heat over medium-high heat just until the mixture comes to a simmer. In a heatproof bowl, whisk together the egg yolks, sugar, vanilla, and salt until doubled in volume, about 2 minutes. Slowly pour about half of the warm cream mixture into the egg mixture, whisking until smooth. Pour the mixture into the saucepan and place over medium heat. Cook, stirring with a wooden spoon, until the mixture thickens enough to coat the back of the spoon, 1–2 minutes. Do not let it boil.

Strain the mixture through a fine-mesh sieve into a bowl and cool completely over an ice bath (see page 14).

If using conventional ice pop molds, divide the mixture among the molds. Cover and freeze until partially frozen, about 1 hour. Using a teaspoon, drop spoonfuls of the firm chocolate mixture into the molds. If using sticks, insert them into the molds at this point. Cover and freeze until solid, at least 3 more hours or up to 3 days.

If using an instant ice pop maker, follow the manufacturer's instructions to fill the molds, adding the chocolate as above, and freeze the pops.

raspberry-chocolate

This recipe calls for creating 3 distinct layers of flavor, alternating the raspberry and chocolate mixtures, but you can change the order or number of layers as desired, partially freezing each layer before adding the next.

2 cups (8 oz/250 g) fresh or frozen raspberries

2 tbsp plus ¼ cup (2 oz/60 g) superfine sugar

Pinch of salt

3 tbsp unsweetened cocoa powder

2 tbsp light corn syrup

¼ cup (2 oz/60 g) sour cream

1 cup (8 fl oz/250 ml) half-and-half

½ cup (4 oz/125 g) vanilla yogurt

MAKES 10–12 ICE POPS

try this
To make cup-shaped ice pops as shown at left, see page 90.

In a blender or food processor, combine the raspberries, 2 tbsp sugar, salt, and 2 tbsp water. Process until very smooth. Pour the raspberry mixture through a fine-mesh sieve set over a large liquid measuring cup and use a flexible spatula to push the liquids through. Discard the seeds.

In a saucepan, combine the ¼ cup sugar, cocoa powder, corn syrup, and sour cream. Bring to a simmer over medium-high heat, stirring until the sugar has completely dissolved. Transfer the mixture to a bowl. Add the half-and-half and yogurt and stir to combine.

If using conventional ice pop molds, fill the molds one-third full with the chocolate mixture and freeze until partially frozen, about 30 minutes. Pour in the raspberry mixture, filling the molds two-thirds full, and again freeze until partially frozen, about 30 minutes. Pour in the remaining chocolate mixture, filling the molds full. If using sticks, insert them into the molds and freeze until solid, at least 3 hours or up to 3 days.

If using an instant ice pop maker, follow the manufacturer's instructions to fill the molds, layering the mixtures as above, and freeze the pops.

mexican chocolate

Mexican chocolate has a good dose of cinnamon to lend a spicy flavor. Here it is used in two forms, both ground and whole, for layers of cinnamon flavor. Rice milk, instead of cow's milk, imparts a frosty, refreshing quality.

2 cups (16 fl oz/500 ml) vanilla-flavored rice milk

1 tbsp unsweetened cocoa powder

1 tbsp packed light brown sugar

1 tbsp granulated sugar

1 cinnamon stick

1/4 tsp ground cinnamon

Pinch of salt

2 oz (60 g) bittersweet chocolate, finely chopped

MAKES 6–9 ICE POPS

In a saucepan over medium-high heat, warm the rice milk, cocoa powder, brown and granulated sugars, cinnamon stick, ground cinnamon, and salt, stirring occasionally until the mixture comes to a boil and the sugar has completely melted. Remove from the heat, add the chopped chocolate, and stir until smooth. Let cool to room temperature. After the mixture has cooled, remove the cinnamon stick.

If using conventional ice pop molds, divide the mixture among the molds. Cover and freeze until solid, at least 4 hours or up to 3 days. If using sticks, insert them into the molds when the pops are partially frozen, after about 1 hour, then freeze until solid, at least 3 hours.

If using an instant ice pop maker, follow the manufacturer's instructions to fill the molds and freeze the pops.

milk chocolate and banana

Both creamy and sweet, the pairing of milk chocolate and bananas is pleasing to everyone, especially kids. This pop layers a yogurt-banana mixture with chocolate to create an attractive two-tone effect.

½ cup (4 fl oz/125 ml) heavy cream

1 tbsp unsweetened cocoa powder

4 oz (60 g) milk chocolate, finely chopped

¾ cup (6 oz/185 g) plain whole-milk yogurt

Pinch of salt

4 firm but ripe bananas, about 2 lb (1 kg) total weight, peeled

1 tbsp superfine sugar

MAKES 10–12 ICE POPS

In a small saucepan over medium-high heat, warm the cream and cocoa powder, stirring occasionally, until the mixture just comes to a simmer. Remove from the heat, add the chopped chocolate, and stir until smooth. Transfer to a bowl and add ¼ cup (2 oz/60 g) of the yogurt and the salt. Stir until completely combined. Let cool to room temperature.

In another bowl, combine the remaining ½ cup (4 oz/125 g) yogurt, the bananas, and the sugar. Use a potato masher to mash the bananas with the yogurt and sugar until a lumpy purée forms.

If using conventional ice pop molds, spoon the banana mixture into molds, filling them one-third full. Freeze until partially frozen, about 30 minutes. Spoon the chocolate mixture on top of the banana mixture, filling the molds two-thirds full. Freeze until partially frozen, about 30 minutes. If using sticks, insert them in the molds at this point. Completely fill the molds with the remaining banana mixture, then cover and freeze until solid, at least 4 hours or up to 3 days.

If using an instant ice pop maker, follow the manufacturer's instructions to fill the molds, layering the mixtures as above, and freeze the pops.

creamy ice pops

orange cream

Orange zest is cooked with orange juice and sugar to give this pop a burst of orange flavor; it is then strained out to maintain a smooth texture. The sour cream gives the pop a silky texture and tangy bite, so it's not too sweet.

1 tbsp finely grated orange zest

2 cups (16 fl oz/500 ml) freshly squeezed orange juice (from about 4 oranges)

1/3 cup (3 oz/90 g) sugar

1 cup (8 fl oz/250 ml) half-and-half

1/2 cup (4 oz/125 g) sour cream

1 tbsp light corn syrup

1/4 cup (2 oz/60 g) plus 1 tbsp superfine sugar

Pinch of salt

MAKES 10–12 ICE POPS

In a heavy saucepan, combine the orange zest and juice and the sugar. Bring to a boil over medium-high heat and cook, stirring occasionally, until the orange juice has reduced to 1 cup (8 fl oz/250 ml), about 7 minutes. Remove from the heat and let cool to room temperature.

In a bowl, whisk together the half-and-half, sour cream, corn syrup, superfine sugar, and salt. Pour the cooled orange mixture into the cream mixture and whisk to combine.

If using conventional ice pop molds, divide the mixture among the molds. Cover and freeze until solid, at least 4 hours or up to 3 days. If using sticks, insert them into the molds when the pops are partially frozen, after about 1 hour, then continue to freeze until solid, at least 3 more hours.

If using an instant ice pop maker, follow the manufacturer's instructions to fill the molds and freeze the pops.

cheesecake

These ice pops taste like frozen cheesecake and are a novel dessert for a casual get-together. For a chocolate crust, substitute chocolate wafer cookies for the graham crackers and crush them in the same manner.

6 graham crackers

1 tbsp sugar plus ¼ cup (2 oz/60 g)

2 tbsp unsalted butter, melted

8 oz (250 g) cream cheese, at room temperature

¼ cup (2 fl oz/60 ml) heavy cream

½ cup (4 fl oz/125 ml) half-and-half

¾ tsp vanilla extract

MAKES 6–9 ICE POPS

Place the graham crackers in a resealable plastic bag and finely crush them using a rolling pin. (You should have about 1 cup/4 oz/125 g of crumbs.) Transfer the crushed graham crackers to a bowl and add the 1 tbsp sugar and melted butter. Stir to mix.

In another bowl, using an electric mixer on medium-high speed, beat the cream cheese until fluffy, about 2 minutes. With the mixer on low speed, gradually add the ¼ cup sugar and beat until smooth, scraping down the sides of the bowl as needed. Add the cream, half-and-half, and vanilla and beat until well blended.

If using conventional ice pop molds, divide the mixture among the molds. Sprinkle 1 tablespoon of the graham cracker mixture evenly over each ice pop, and press gently to adhere the crumbs to the pop. Cover and freeze until solid, at least 4 hours or up to 3 days. If using sticks, insert them into the molds when the pops are partially frozen, after about 1 hour, then continue to freeze until solid, at least 3 more hours.

If using an instant ice pop maker, follow the manufacturer's instructions to fill the molds, adding the crumbs as above, and freeze the pops.

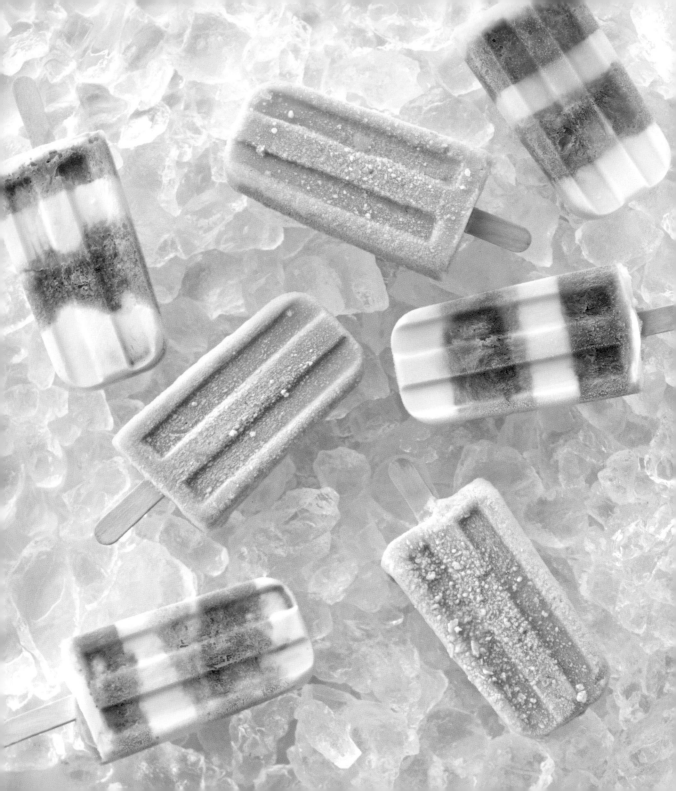

root beer cream

The layers of frozen root beer and vanilla custard will remind you of the soda-fountain favorite, root beer float. Open the root beer at least 30 minutes before use so that the carbonation doesn't create a mess in your freezer.

1 cup (8 fl oz/250 ml) heavy cream

1 cup (8 fl oz/250 ml) whole milk

4 large egg yolks

1/3 cup (3 oz/90 g) sugar

1 tsp vanilla extract

Pinch of salt

2 cups (16 fl oz/500 ml) root beer

MAKES 12–14 ICE POPS

In a heavy saucepan over medium-high heat, warm the cream and milk until the mixture just comes to a simmer, about 5 minutes. In a heatproof bowl, whisk together the egg yolks, sugar, vanilla, and salt until doubled in volume, about 2 minutes. Slowly pour about half of the warm cream mixture into the egg mixture, whisking until smooth. Pour the mixture into the saucepan and place over medium heat. Cook, stirring with a wooden spoon, until the mixture thickens enough to coat the back of the spoon, 1–2 minutes. Do not let it boil. Strain through a fine-mesh sieve into a bowl. Cool completely over an ice bath (see page 14).

If using conventional ice pop molds, fill the molds one-fourth full with the vanilla mixture and freeze until partially frozen, about 30 minutes. Pour in the root beer, filling the molds until they are half full, and again freeze until partially frozen, about 30 minutes. Pour in the remaining vanilla mixture, filling the molds three-fourths full. If using sticks, insert them into the molds and freeze until almost completely solid, about 1 hour. Fill the molds with the remaining root beer. Cover and freeze until solid, at least 2½ hours or up to 3 days. (It is not recommended to use carbonated beverages in instant ice pop makers.)

ALSO SHOWN: PEACHES AND CREAM ICE POPS (PAGE 63)

meyer lemon cream

The floral fragrance of a Meyer lemon, a cross between traditional lemon and mandarin, gives these ice pops an alluring appeal. These creamy, smooth pops combine the tang of lemons with the sweet richness of condensed milk.

1 tbsp Meyer lemon zest

¾ cup (6 fl oz/180 ml) Meyer lemon juice (from about 5 lemons)

1 can (14 oz/440 g) sweetened condensed milk

½ cup (4 fl oz/125 ml) heavy cream

Pinch of salt

MAKES 8–10 ICE POPS

In a bowl, stir together the lemon zest and juice, condensed milk, cream, and salt until well blended.

If using conventional ice pop molds, divide the mixture among the molds. Cover and freeze until solid, at least 4 hours or up to 3 days. If using sticks, insert them into the molds when the pops are partially frozen, after about 1 hour, then continue to freeze until solid, at least 3 more hours.

If using an instant ice pop maker, follow the manufacturer's instructions to fill the molds and freeze the pops.

peaches and cream

Peaches are sweet and juicy on their own, but when blended with half-and-half and frozen, the result is an ice pop that is both thirst quenching and luxurious. Plain whole-milk yogurt can be used in place of the half-and-half, if desired.

3 ripe peaches, about
1 lb (500 g) total weight

1/3 cup (3 oz/90 g)
superfine sugar

2 tsp freshly squeezed
lemon juice

1/3 cup (3 fl oz/80 ml)
half-and-half

Pinch of salt

MAKES 8–10 ICE POPS

Bring a saucepan of water to a boil. Cut a shallow X in the blossom end of each peach. Lower the peaches into the boiling water and let stand for about 30 seconds. Using a slotted spoon, transfer the peaches to a bowl. When cool enough to handle, use a paring knife to peel the skin from each fruit, beginning at the X. Halve the peaches and remove the pits. Roughly chop the peach flesh.

In a blender or food processor, combine the peaches, sugar, lemon juice, half-and-half, and salt. Process until completely smooth.

If using conventional ice pop molds, divide the mixture among the molds. Cover and freeze until solid, at least 4 hours or up to 3 days. If using sticks, insert them into the molds when the pops are partially frozen, after about 1 hour, then continue to freeze until solid, at least 3 more hours.

If using an instant ice pop maker, follow the manufacturer's instructions to fill the molds and freeze the pops.

strawberry-vanilla swirl

Sweet and fragrant, fresh strawberries are a nice match for the tangy vanilla yogurt in this springtime pop. Using whole-milk yogurt gives these pops an especially creamy texture, but lowfat yogurt can also be substituted.

2½ cups (10 oz/315 g) strawberries, hulled and cut in half

2 tbsp superfine sugar

1 tsp freshly squeezed lemon juice

Pinch of salt

1½ cups (12 oz/375 g) vanilla whole-milk yogurt

MAKES 12–14 ICE POPS

In a blender or food processor, combine the strawberries, sugar, lemon juice, and salt. Process until completely smooth.

If using conventional ice pop molds, place 2 tbsp of the yogurt in each ice pop mold. Top each with 2 tbsp of the strawberry mixture. Continue layering the yogurt and strawberry mixture in the molds until the molds are full. Dip a paring knife into each mold and make a few figure-eight motions to swirl the flavors together. Cover and freeze until solid, at least 4 hours or up to 3 days. If using sticks, insert them in the molds when the pops are partially frozen, after about 1 hour, then continue to freeze until solid, at least 3 more hours.

If using an instant ice pop maker, follow the manufacturer's instructions to fill the molds, layering the mixtures as above, and freeze the pops.

coconut-cinnamon

Cinnamon adds a surprising twist to this decadent ice pop. To maintain the creamy texture, avoid substituting light coconut milk. For a creative presentation, try inserting a cinnamon stick (see page 86) in place of other sticks.

1 cup (8 fl oz/250 ml) heavy cream

1/4 cup (1 oz/30 g) plus 2 tbsp confectioners' sugar

1 can (13 1/2 oz/425 g) coconut milk

1/2 cup (2 oz/60 g) sweetened shredded coconut

1/2 cup (4 fl oz/125 ml) whole milk

3/4 teaspoon ground cinnamon

MAKES 10–12 ICE POPS

In a chilled bowl, combine the cream and sugar. Using an electric mixer on low speed, beat until slightly thickened, 1–2 minutes. Gradually increase the speed to medium-high and continue to beat until the cream holds soft peaks, 2–3 minutes.

In a blender, combine the coconut milk and shredded coconut. Process until the mixture is mostly smooth. Transfer to a 4-cup (32–fl oz/1-l) measure with a pour spout. Stir in the milk and cinnamon. Gently whisk in the whipped cream.

If using conventional ice pop molds, divide the mixture among the molds. Cover and freeze until solid, at least 4 hours or up to 3 days. If using sticks, insert them in the molds when the pops are partially frozen, after about 1 hour, then freeze until solid, at least 3 hours.

If using an instant ice pop maker, follow the manufacturer's instructions to fill the molds and freeze the pops.

cherry-honey-yogurt swirl

The color of Bing cherries ranges from deep garnet to almost black, but the flesh is always firm and sweet. Available in early spring through summer, their nice balance of tart and sweet flavors is nicely showcased in an ice pop.

½ lb (250 g) fresh or frozen Bing cherries, halved and pitted

½ cup (6 oz/180 g) honey

1 tsp freshly squeezed lemon juice

1¾ cup (14 oz/440 g) plain whole-milk yogurt

¾ cup (6 fl oz/180 ml) whole milk

MAKES 10–12 ICE POPS

In a saucepan, combine the cherries, ¼ cup (3 oz/90 g) of the honey, and the lemon juice. Bring to a simmer over medium-high heat and cook, stirring occasionally, until the liquid has reduced and thickened to syrup consistency, about 5 minutes. Remove the mixture from the heat and let cool to room temperature.

In a 4-cup (32–fl oz/1-l) measure with a pour spout, stir together the yogurt, milk, and remaining ¼ cup honey. Add the cooled cherry mixture and gently swirl to combine, leaving large streaks.

If using conventional ice pop molds, divide the mixture among the molds. Cover and freeze until solid, at least 4 hours or up to 3 days. If using sticks, insert them in the molds when the pops are partially frozen, after about 1 hour, then freeze until solid, at least 3 more hours.

If using an instant ice pop maker, follow the manufacturer's instructions to fill the molds and freeze the pops.

caramel-almond

¾ cup (6 oz/185 g) sugar

2 tbsp unsalted butter

1½ cups (12 fl oz/375 ml) whole milk

1½ cups (12 fl oz/375 ml) heavy cream

5 large egg yolks

½ tsp almond extract

½ tsp vanilla extract

Pinch of salt

MAKES 10–12 ICE POPS

pop swap
For chocolate–nut crunch ice pops, dip the finished ice pops into melted chocolate and then immediately into crushed nut brittle. Place on a parchment-lined baking sheet and freeze until ready to serve.

In a heavy saucepan over medium-high heat, warm the sugar, stirring constantly, until it begins to melt, about 5 minutes. Cook, stirring, until the sugar melts and turns golden amber, about 3 minutes. Stirring constantly, carefully add the butter, milk, and cream. Reduce the heat to medium and cook, stirring, until the mixture is completely smooth and returns to a bare simmer, about 5 minutes. Remove from the heat.

In a heatproof bowl, whisk together the egg yolks, almond and vanilla extracts, and salt until doubled in volume, about 2 minutes. Slowly pour about half of the warm milk mixture into the egg mixture, whisking until smooth. Pour the mixture into the saucepan and place over medium heat. Cook, stirring with a wooden spoon, until the mixture thickens enough to coat the back of the spoon, 1–2 minutes. Do not let it boil.

Strain the mixture through a fine-mesh sieve into a bowl and cool completely over an ice bath (see page 14).

If using conventional ice pop molds, divide the mixture among the molds. Cover and freeze until solid, at least 4 hours or up to 3 days. If using sticks, insert them in the molds when the pops are partially frozen, after about 1 hour, then freeze until solid, at least 3 more hours.

If using an instant ice pop maker, follow the manufacturer's instructions to fill the molds and freeze the pops.

vanilla–toffee chip

This recipe starts with an easy custard made from whole milk, egg yolks, and intensely flavored vanilla seeds. Bits of toffee are added to the cooled custard before freezing, creating candy bar–like appeal in an ice pop.

2 cups (16 fl oz/500 ml) whole milk

1½ tbsp cornstarch

1 large egg plus 3 large egg yolks

¾ cup (6 oz/185 g) sugar

Pinch of salt

½ vanilla bean, split in half lengthwise

½ cup (3 oz/90 g) toffee pieces

MAKES 10–12 ICE POPS

In a heavy saucepan, combine 1½ cups (12 fl oz/375 ml) of the milk and the cornstarch. Bring to a boil over medium-high heat and cook, stirring occasionally, until the mixture has thickened, 7–10 minutes. Meanwhile, in a bowl, whisk together the remaining ½ cup milk, and the whole egg and egg yolks, sugar, and salt. Using a knife, scrape the seeds from the vanilla bean halves into the bowl and then add the halves. Stirring constantly, add the egg mixture to the thickened milk mixture. Cook, whisking constantly, over medium-high heat until the mixture returns to a boil. Remove from the heat.

Pour the custard through a fine-mesh sieve into a bowl, then cool over an ice bath (see page 14). Stir the toffee pieces into the cooled custard.

If using conventional ice pop molds, divide the mixture among the molds. Cover and freeze until solid, at least 6 hours or up to 3 days. If using sticks, insert them in the molds when the pops are partially frozen, after about 1 hour, then freeze until solid, at least 5 more hours.

If using an instant ice pop maker, follow the manufacturer's instructions to fill the molds and freeze the pops.

cookies and cream

Reminiscent of an ice-cream sandwich, this pop mingles dark chocolate cookie pieces in a creamy vanilla base. The small amount of sour cream lends rich texture and just a hint of tanginess to offset the pops' sweet flavors.

14 chocolate wafer cookies, about 4 oz (125 g) total weight

¼ cup (2 oz/60 g) superfine sugar

½ cup (4 fl oz/125 ml) sour cream

¼ cup (2 fl oz/60 ml) whole milk

1 cup (8 fl oz/250 ml) heavy cream

1 tsp vanilla extract

MAKES 8–10 ICE POPS

Working over a small bowl, crumble the cookies to make pieces about the size of peas.

In a bowl, stir together the sugar and ¼ cup (2 fl oz/60 ml) water until the sugar has completely dissolved. Stir in the sour cream, milk, cream, and vanilla. Add the crumbled chocolate cookies and stir to mix.

If using conventional ice pop molds, divide the mixture among the molds. Cover and freeze until solid, at least 4 hours or up to 3 days. If using sticks, insert them into the molds when the pops are partially frozen, after about 1 hour, then freeze until solid, at least 3 more hours.

If using an instant ice pop maker, follow the manufacturer's instructions to fill the molds and freeze the pops.

pop swap
Use your favorite cookie in place of the chocolate wafers. Try oatmeal, chocolate chip, or ginger snap.

o new flavors for ice pops

cappuccino

Taking your coffee in a frozen state is an interesting variation on the classic hot cappuccino. All of the usual components are included in this coffee-flavored pop, even the foamy cap. Dust the top with cinnamon or nutmeg, if you like.

1¾ cups (14 fl oz/430 ml) strongly brewed coffee

⅓ cup (3 fl oz/80 ml) whole milk

¼ cup (2 oz/60 g) superfine sugar

¼ cup (2 fl oz/60 ml) heavy cream

1 tsp confectioners' sugar

MAKES 6–8 ICE POPS

pop swap
For mocha ice pops, whisk 2 tbsp sweetened hot cocoa mix into the coffee mixture when adding the sugar.

In a 4-cup (32–fl oz/1-l) measure with a pour spout, combine the coffee, milk, and superfine sugar. Stir until the sugar has completely dissolved. Set aside. In a bowl, combine the cream and confectioners' sugar. Using a whisk, beat until the cream forms soft peaks. Set aside.

If using conventional ice pop molds, divide the coffee mixture among the molds, then spoon a dollop of the whipped cream into each mold. Cover and freeze until solid, at least 4 hours or up to 3 days. If using sticks, insert them into the molds when the pops are partially frozen, after about 1 hour, then freeze until solid, at least 3 more hours.

If using an instant ice pop maker, follow the manufacturer's instructions to fill the molds, layering the mixtures as above, and freeze the pops.

green tea–pomegranate

This ice pop is packed with antioxidants, both from the green tea and the red pomegranate seeds. Healthful qualities aside, these pops have a lightly sweet flavor and beautiful color combination that are sure to please.

¼ cup (2 oz/60 g) sugar

3 bags green tea

1½ tsp freshly squeezed lemon juice

1 tbsp clover honey, or to taste (optional)

½ cup (2 oz/60 g) pomegranate seeds (from 1 small pomegranate)

MAKES 6–10 ICE POPS

In a saucepan, combine the sugar and 2 cups (16 fl oz/500 ml) water. Bring to a boil over medium-high heat, stirring occasionally, until the sugar has completely dissolved. Remove from the heat and let cool for 5 minutes. Add the tea bags and let steep until the tea has cooled to room temperature. Remove and discard the tea bags and transfer the tea to a 4-cup (16–fl oz/500-ml) measure with a pour spout. Add the lemon juice and the honey, if using.

If using conventional ice pop molds, divide the pomegranate seeds evenly among the molds. Pour the green tea mixture into each mold just to cover the seeds. When the pops are partially frozen, after about 1 hour, pour the remaining green tea mixture into the molds to fill. Freeze until solid, at least 3 hours. If using sticks, insert them into the molds when the pops are partially frozen, about 1 hour, then freeze until solid, at least 3 more hours.

If using an instant ice pop maker, follow the manufacturer's instructions to fill the molds, layering the mixtures as above, and freeze the pops.

orange-blackberry sangria

2 oranges

One 750-ml bottle light dry fruity red wine such as Rioja or Beaujolais

¼ cup (2 oz/60 g) plus 2 tbsp sugar

1 small tart green apple such as Granny Smith, peeled, cored, and cut into ½-inch (12-mm) pieces

1 cup (4 oz/125 g) blackberries

Pinch of salt

MAKES 12–14 ICE POPS

try this
Cut thin slices of apple, brush them with lemon juice, and thread onto the stick to use as a drip guard.

Using a vegetable peeler, remove 5 wide strips of zest from 1 orange. Juice the fruit and strain into a measuring cup. You should have ⅓ cup (3 fl oz/80 ml). Cut the top and bottom from the remaining orange. Set the orange upright and, following the contour of the fruit, cut off the peel, pith, and membrane. Holding the orange over a bowl, cut along each side of the membranes between the sections. Let the sections fall into the bowl along with any juice. Cut the sections into ½-inch (12-mm) pieces. Strain the juice into the measuring cup or reserve for another use.

Pour the wine into a saucepan and bring to a boil over medium-high heat. Reduce the heat to low and simmer until reduced to 2 cups (16 fl oz/ 500 ml), about 5 minutes. Add the sugar, orange juice, orange zest, orange pieces, apple pieces, blackberries, and salt. Pour in 6 tbsp (3 fl oz/90 ml) water. Stir until the sugar has completely dissolved. Remove from heat and let cool to room temperature.

If using conventional ice pop molds, divide the mixture evenly among the molds, ensuring each has about the same amount of fruit. Cover and freeze until solid, at least 4 hours or up to 3 days. If using sticks, insert them in the molds when the pops are partially frozen, after about 1 hour, then freeze until firm, at least 3 more hours.

If using an instant ice pop maker, follow the manufacturer's instructions to fill the molds and freeze the pops.

apple cider

One bite of this pop will remind you of sipping mulled cider on a crisp autumn day. Unfiltered apple cider, with its intense apple flavor, is a better choice for these pops than the typical filtered apple juice from grocery stores.

3 cups (24 fl oz/750 ml) unfiltered apple cider

1 cinnamon stick

2 whole allspice berries

2 strips orange zest, each about 1 inch (2.5 cm) wide and 3 inches (7.5 cm) long

1 whole clove

2 tbsp sugar

1 1/4 tsp apple cider vinegar or freshly squeezed lemon juice

Pinch of salt

MAKES 8–10 ICE POPS

In a saucepan, combine the apple cider, cinnamon stick, allspice, orange zest, clove, and sugar. Bring to a boil over medium-high heat and cook, stirring occasionally, until the sugar has completely dissolved and the spices smell very fragrant, about 5 minutes. Remove from the heat and let cool to room temperature.

Strain the mixture into a 4-cup (32–fl oz/1-l) measure with a pour spout. Add the vinegar and salt and stir to combine.

If using conventional ice pop molds, divide the mixture among the molds. Cover and freeze until solid, at least 4 hours or up to 3 days. If using sticks, insert them into the molds when the pops are partially frozen, after about 1 hour, then freeze until solid, at least 3 more hours.

If using an instant ice pop maker, follow the manufacturer's instructions to fill the molds and freeze the pops.

mimosa

Usually an adult cocktail served with brunch, a Mimosa is typically made from equal parts sparkling wine and orange juice. This ice pop uses a bit less sparkling wine than the cocktail so that the alcohol won't hinder the freezing process.

1¾ cups (14 fl oz/430 ml) freshly squeezed orange juice (from about 6 oranges)

¾ cup (6 fl oz/180 ml) sparkling wine

3 tbsp superfine sugar

MAKES 8–10 ICE POPS

In a 4-cup (32–fl oz/1-l) measure with a pour spout, stir together the orange juice, sparkling wine, and sugar until well mixed and the sugar has completely dissolved.

If using conventional ice pop molds, divide the mixture among the molds. Cover and freeze until solid, at least 8 hours or up to 3 days. If using sticks, insert them into the molds when the pops are partially frozen, after about 2 hours, then freeze until solid, at least 6 more hours. (It is not recommended to use carbonated beverages in instant ice pop makers.)

cucumber-lime-mint

The cool and refreshing combination of cucumber, lime, and mint will surprise and delight all ice pop lovers. A perfect way to beat the heat in the summer, these ice pops are elegant enough to impress and far too delicious to resist.

½ cup (4 oz/125 g) sugar

1 English cucumber, cut crosswise into thin slices

½ cup (4 fl oz/125 ml) freshly squeezed lime juice

¼ cup (¼ oz/7 g) fresh mint leaves

1 tsp finely grated lime zest

MAKES 8–10 ICE POPS

pop swap
To turn this pop into a frozen cocktail, add ¼ cup (2 fl oz/60 ml) vodka or gin to the strained cucumber mixture. Increase the freezing time to 5 hours.

In a saucepan, combine the sugar, half of the cucumber slices (about 20), the lime juice, and the mint leaves. Pour in 1¾ cups (14 fl oz/430 ml) water. Bring to a boil over medium-high heat, stirring occasionally, until the sugar has dissolved. Remove from the heat and let cool to room temperature.

Strain the cucumber mixture into a 4-cup (32–fl oz/1-l) measure with a pour spout. Add the lime zest and stir to combine.

If using conventional ice pop molds, divide the cucumber mixture among the molds. Then, divide the remaining cucumber slices among the molds, using a stick to push the slices down into the molds. Cover and freeze until solid, at least 4 hours or up to 3 days. If using sticks, insert them into the molds when the pops are partially frozen, after about 1 hour, then freeze until solid, at least 3 more hours.

If using an instant ice pop maker, follow the manufacturer's instructions to fill the molds, adding the cucumber slices as above, and freeze the pops.

lavender-huckleberry

Typically available from late July through August, huckleberries have a delicious tang and striking deep purple hue, which is complemented here by sweet, floral lavender. If huckleberries are unavailable, substitute fresh or frozen blackberries.

½ cup (4 oz/125 g) sugar

1½ tsp pesticide-free fresh lavender blossoms, or ¾ teaspoon dried lavender

Zest of 1 lemon, removed in thin strips

¼ cup (1 oz/30 g) fresh or frozen huckleberries

⅓ cup (3 fl oz/80 ml) freshly squeezed lemon juice (from about 3 lemons)

MAKES 8–10 ICE POPS

In a saucepan, combine the sugar, lavender, and lemon zest strips. Pour in ½ cup (4 fl oz/125 ml) water. Bring to a boil over medium-high heat, stirring occasionally, until the sugar has completely dissolved and a syrup has formed. Lightly crush the berries with a fork. Add the berries to the syrup, remove from the heat, and let stand for 5 minutes. Strain the mixture through a fine-mesh sieve, into a 4-cup (32–fl oz/1-l) measure with a pour spout. Add the lemon juice and 1 cup (8 fl oz/250 ml) water and stir to combine. Let cool to room temperature.

If using conventional ice pop molds, divide the mixture among the molds. Cover and freeze until solid, at least 4 hours or up to 3 days. If using sticks, insert them into the molds when the pops are partially frozen, after about 1 hour, then freeze until solid, at least 3 more hours.

If using an instant ice pop maker, follow the manufacturer's instructions to fill the molds and freeze the pops.

chai tea

Chai, originating in India, is a blend of black tea and spices often served hot with milk and sugar. Here, whole spices are simmered with Darjeeling tea and then added to milk, replicating the flavors of traditional chai tea in an ice pop.

¼ cup (2 oz/60 g) plus 2 tbsp sugar

2 bags Darjeeling or other black tea

1 cinnamon stick

6 whole cloves

8 green cardamom pods, cracked with the side of a knife

6 peppercorns

1-inch (2.5-cm) piece fresh ginger, peeled and thinly sliced

¾ cup (6 fl oz/180 ml) whole milk

MAKES 8–10 ICE POPS

try this
Insert cinnamon sticks in place of regular ice pop sticks.

In a saucepan, combine the sugar, tea bags, cinnamon stick, cloves, cardamom, peppercorns, and ginger. Pour in 2 cups (16 fl oz/500 ml) water. Bring to a simmer over medium-high heat, stirring occasionally, until the sugar has completely dissolved. Remove the mixture from the heat and let cool to room temperature.

Strain the mixture into a 4-cup (32–fl oz/1-l) measure with a pour spout. Stir in the milk until blended.

If using conventional ice pop molds, divide the mixture among the molds. Cover and freeze until solid, at least 4 hours or up to 3 days. If using sticks, insert them in the molds when the pops are partially frozen, after about 1 hour, then freeze until solid, at least 3 more hours.

If using an instant ice pop maker, follow the manufacturer's instructions to fill the molds and freeze the pops.

strawberry-basil

The slight anise flavor of sweet basil contributes a wonderful fragrance to the strawberries in this ice pop. Both strawberries and basil emerge from the garden early in the summer and are easy to find in the market at the same time.

⅓ cup (3 fl oz/80 ml) sugar

⅓ cup (⅓ oz/10 g) fresh basil leaves, roughly chopped

2½ cups (10 oz/315 g) strawberries, hulled and cut in half

1 tsp freshly squeezed lemon juice

Pinch of salt

MAKES 10–12 ICE POPS

try this
To make ice pops in silicone cupcake cups, turn to page 90.

In a small saucepan, combine the sugar and basil. Pour in ⅓ cup (3 fl oz/ 80 ml) water. Bring to a boil over medium-high heat, stirring occasionally, until the sugar has completely dissolved and a syrup has formed. Remove from the heat and let cool to room temperature.

Using a fine-mesh sieve, strain the basil syrup into a blender or food processor, discarding the basil leaves. Add the strawberry halves, lemon juice, and salt. Process until very smooth.

If using conventional ice pop molds, divide the mixture among the molds. Cover and freeze until solid, at least 4 hours or up to 3 days. If using sticks, insert them into the molds when the pops are partially frozen, after about 1 hour, then freeze until solid, at least 3 more hours.

If using an instant ice pop maker, follow the manufacturer's instructions to fill the molds and freeze the pops.

creative shapes

Ice pop molds are available in a variety of shapes and sizes, but you don't need to rely on special equipment to make the frozen treats. A variety of kitchen items can be used to mold ice pops into interesting, often whimsical, forms.

baking molds Pour the pop mixture into small fluted or regular metal molds, cover, and freeze until partially firm, about 1 hour. Insert sticks, cover and freeze until completely firm, about 3 hours. Let the molds stand at room temperature for about 5 minutes, then pull on the sticks to unmold. If pops are stuck, quickly run the metal portion of the mold under warm water and pull on the sticks to remove the pops.

drinking glasses Pour the pop mixture into drinking glasses, cover, and freeze until partially firm, about 1 hour. Insert sticks, cover, and freeze until completely firm, about 3 hours. Let the glasses stand at room temperature for about 5 minutes, then gently pull on the sticks to unmold. If the pops are stuck, quickly run the glass portion of the mold under warm water and pull on the sticks again to remove the pops.

bar-shaped molds Line a loaf pan with parchment paper so it overhangs the sides. Pour the mixture into the pan, cover, and freeze until firm, about 3 hours. Lift out the mixture, and cut crosswise into 8 pieces. Insert the sticks if desired, using a knife to create a slit, and return to the freezer until solid, about 1 more hour.

cup-shaped molds Pour the pop mixture into paper cups, cover, and freeze until partially firm, about 1 hour. Insert sticks, cover, and freeze until completely firm, about 3 hours. Peel the paper cup off of the pop to unmold.

silicone cupcake cups Pour the pop mixture into silicone cake cups. Cover and freeze until partially firm, about 1 hour. Insert sticks, cover, and freeze until completely firm, about 3 hours. Carefully pull on the sticks to remove the pops.

index

weldonowen

415 Jackson Street, Suite 200, San Francisco, CA 94111
Telephone: 415 291 0100 Fax: 415 291 8841
www.weldonowen.com

WELDON OWEN INC.

CEO and President Terry Newell
Senior VP, International Sales Stuart Laurence
VP, Sales and New Business Development Amy Kaneko
Director of Finance Mark Perrigo

VP and Publisher Hannah Rahill
Executive Editor Jennifer Newens
Editor Donita Boles
Associate Editor Julia Humes
Editorial Assistant Becky Duffett

Associate Creative Director Emma Boys
Art Director Alexandra Zeigler
Junior Designer Anna Grace

Production Director Chris Hemesath
Production Manager Michelle Duggan
Color Manager Teri Bell

Group Publisher, Bonnier Publishing Group John Owen

Photographer Lauren Burke
Food Stylist Shelly Kaldunski
Prop Stylist Christine Wolheim

ICE POPS

Conceived and produced by Weldon Owen Inc.
Copyright © 2010 Weldon Owen Inc.

All rights reserved, including the right of reproduction
in whole or in part in any form.

Color separations by Embassy Graphics
Printed and bound in China by 1010 Printing International Ltd.
First printed in 2010
10 9 8 7 6 5 4 3 2 1

Library of Congress Cataloging-in-Publication
data is available.

ISBN-13: 978-1-61628-010-9
ISBN-10: 1-61628-010-7

ACKNOWLEDGMENTS

Weldon Owen wishes to thank the following people for their generous support in producing this book:
Ara Armstrong, Judith Dunham, Sean Franzen, Lauren Harwell, and Lesli Neilson.